# Split Scre

## *Poems Inspired by*

**Edited by Andy Jackson**

**Red Squirrel Press**

First published in the UK in 2012 by
Red Squirrel Press
Briery Hill Cottage
Stannington
Morpeth
Northumberland
United Kingdom
NE61 6ES
www.redsquirrelpress.com

Red Squirrel Press is represented by Inpress Ltd.
www.inpressbooks.co.uk

Cover design by Paul Mawson

A CIP catalogue record is available from the British Library
ISBN: 978-1-906700-60-7

Printed by Martins the Printers
Sea View Works
Spittal
Berwick-upon-Tweed
United Kingdom
TD15 1RS

# Acknowledgments

Some poems in this collection have previously appeared in other publications. Thanks go to their editors for allowing us to use them.

The editor would like to thank the following for their advice and enthusiasm:- the indefatigable Kevin Cadwallender and the eternally patient Sheila Wakefield at Red Squirrel Press, Simon Barraclough, Mark Burnhope, Brian Johnstone, AB Jackson, Tim Wells, WN Herbert and Jo Bell. Thanks also to Tim Turnbull and Chris Emery for the initial inspiration – you had no idea what you were starting!

Naturally, thanks go to all the excellent writers who have contributed poems, ideas or support for the Split Screen project.

Particular thanks go to Paul Mawson for his rather wonderful cover art.

For Leslie Halliwell

# Contents

## Camberwick Green

Episode over, it's not
over. He's always there,
present and correct:

the boy-pierrot,
his clothes-peg head,
body of sponge,

in slow mechanical
motion or mouse-toil,
a workhouse gavotte:

he turns and again turns
a wooden crank handle,
that's all, a repeat

action which rolls up
a ream of credits:
voice, animation,

those responsible …
he stops at each name,
regards them, unreading,

his blank intervals.
Elsewhere, off camera,
the goodmorning Green

continues: busy bees
wriggle and share news,
the police constable

trills his usual song,
a miller grinds corn …
but here, this final

turn, this wind-up task,
and him surrounded
by antique lute,

untouchable school bell,
military drum, where
*is* this, The End, half

attic room, half stage;
what had he done
wrong, the child,

star of loneliness.

*AB Jackson*

## Tiny Clanger Tanka

True, I'm born of wool
and live my life in stop-frame,
yet, remember this:
my every word is music
and I am heir to planets

*Alan Smithee*

## Champion

Now, what possessed your seven-year-old self
to moon so, for Alexandra Bastedo,
the home-grown, surrogate Bardot of Hove,
like an inchoate Young Werther? Heartfelt
it was, though inexpressible as yet,
clipping out the Titbits pictures and, *Oh!*
sigh at each new coiffure, each swimsuit pose,
burn, boy in anticipation of hells
to be endured, the sweet agonies to come
and Stuart Damon's gorgeous, gorgeous eyes,
perfect hair, suit, pocket square – it's killer,
nearly Perkins, man. Life won't be humdrum
while we've such models. So hurry, time flies,
bring on the love interest, pass the mirror.

*Tim Turnbull*

## Guest Starring

When I look back on those dossier-rich years, the brown packages
and latex cheeks, jet-fuming plans over arrogant sand, the dark cages
of Lubyanka, the high-kicking generalissimos in Colombia,
Mafia-hosted hoe-downs and all that Cold War paraphernalia,

what I never got was Willy: the gibbon with the giant neck.
What was it with the silent treatment, Jim? Was he a total wreck?
But then, what has the ass-whupping, Commie-smashing whole farrago
got to do with *our* America? I'm still in two minds about the show.

Did you ever fancy that each repetitious script
was just some pretext for the counter-counter culture? A crypt-
ic stab at hawkish new imperialism? Anyway, the seventh season
sorted all the Sam Browne-belted Slavs. I guess we always won.

Unmasked or Frenchified, the whole thing trimmed and canned
like that. Cinnamon's objectified ass. Rollin's sleight of hand.
Barney sweating over dials and knobs. Who thought it would outlast
the KGB, the Stasi and the rest, with such an over-earnest cast?

I have this dream of elevator shafts, tunnels, drain pipes, heights;
misdirected collapsing that ruptures into fights.
You know, I never would have left but for some extra's crappy joke:
*some lives are like a burning fuse, but yours is just a puff of smoke.*

*Chris Emery*

## Fanfic

He's a fan, all right,
but he steers clear of fan sites on the Internet.

Years ago, he happened across
some Blake/Avon slash, and he was horrified –

not, he swears, at the homoerotic content.
It was the disrespect to Terry Nation's IPR that shook him.

And I may not have helped, saying
*Of course they were.*

*Couldn't you tell?*
I had to make his Valentine that year

a photo of Servalan in a red dress,
just to make it up to him.

But thinking about it now, I think
I spoke the truth unwittingly:

that there was a love of some kind,
on Avon's side at any rate.

Look how he reacted when he thought
love had betrayed him.

I don't say that to my love though.
He'd be horrified all over again,
and not at Blake or Avon.

*Judith Taylor*

## A Job Down Mexico Way

Chris, I stayed in but you have not come
though I know you need good men
a pleiad for a job down Mexico way.

Bandidos have plundered
the beautiful rhymes of harvest
left the villagers hungry.

Those poor peasant farmers
powerless against the might of Calvera
his speeches of slow rambling prose.

I'm sure you've started already
recruiting somebody sharp tongued
quick on the lyrical draw

a second — a builder of sonnets
to strengthen defences
another handy with a haiku.

There's always one who is good
with children — light verse at bed time
and a tortured soul haunted by terza rima.

But surely there is room for one more
an ageing versenary who can disarm
with a perfectly chosen phrase.

It is not about the money
I'm a poet after all – it's about my craft
One last job – one last stanza.

Chris, I long for your smile at my door
for you to hold up seven fingers
for us to ride out in a short line at dawn.

*Jim Carruth*

## Whom Fate Has Made Indestructible

The first few times it felt like being swallowed:
the dynamite just out of reach, then bells
as loud as his own livery that bellowed
and slugged him back beyond their bronze glottals.
Caught between the tank track and mud-weals,
his splitting bones awoke the earth's chilled tongue,
which muscled all the shreds of him in schools
down an oesophagus of root and song.

But chewed or roasted, served as mash or salad,
he couldn't be kept down. Death's stomach walls
convulsed, caved in and brought him back, unhalo'd,
fresh and whole from his stubble to his smalls.
So over time, his bloody, brief farewells
became a sort of furious thrill. He flung
himself into the lairs of animals,
the paths of missiles, fireballs, jaws that sprung,

and sometimes made it out with one cut eyelid
to wild relief, promotion, lovestruck girls.
If instead he ended up marshmallowed,
or steaked, or pancaked, all the better. Lulls
in mortal peril worked his heart like mills
and days without demise stretched on too long.
Sleepless, he developed rituals
of falling, frying, gas, self-poisoning.

Now watch him from the launch. Seawater swells
around him as he sinks into a lung
of shrinking light, a thousand funerals
moving through his mind like so much slang.

*Jon Stone*

14

# UFO

Bodies in the green gel wrappers
in the closed and corrugated carriages

skins crumpled from the long years of sleep
lips twisted like folded back sheets

over bluish gumshields, the tongues
protected for the flight.

Bodies of the travellers, taken to revival stations,
columnated, singled out in fenced-off grassless zones

between the disused flyovers
behind the sunken railway arches where the homeless crouch

among the containers graffittied years ago and left,
their cargos liquified, beneath

the perpetual evening of a tiny distant sun
which thin strips of two-tone clouds —

pearl and salmon — can lose
along their gloaming lengths for months.

Engineless, the carriage rolls as though there is a slope
too imperceptible for any gravity but ours

a slight incline that stretches from this tree
in search of its blossomless mate.

*W N Herbert*

## The Dark Days Are Done

You were shot full of holes before you started.
A study in cinematic teleology,
you hearkened to the rat-a-tat-tat of your father's footsteps
from your bassinet, felt the landlord's knuckles *bang-bang,*
*you're dead* rap like premonitions while you slept
long before you learned to hit the sack and far too early to fight back.

So true to the principles, Principe, of those holy codes
of honour, business, chivalry, sewn-up like coins in the lining
of your American immigrant dream of daughters and sons,
dollars and cents, democracy, the mob, the family,
that that one big seducing, dubious idea didn't even have to try
to justify its life through you, who were and weren't your father's son.

So why were you so angry, and why was anyone surprised
there wasn't a lickspittle of you left, plumb riddled with the jokes
Barzinis would shoot each other across the lasagna down
the generations forever: *What's got a thousand eyes and mouths*
*and ears—and cannot talk or see or hear? Whaddya get*
*when you cross a* pazzo *bull with forty rounds of provolone?*

Sonny boy, you never had a chance, and maybe that's why,
bully and brute though you were through and through,
we always hate to see you go. Sun-shafted as a Sicilian barn.
Hooked and jerked and rooted to the spot like a boneless fish
in a stocked pond. You never knew what hit you.
You never did, like Leda may have done, take it off and put it on.

And when he says, *Look how they massacred my boy,*
we all forget, seeing you grinning like Icarus in your suspenders,
the son who soared until he roared up to the fiery gates of hell,
how your archangel double darkened, hardened, soured, fell.

*Liane Strauss*

16

## Godfather

So Michael, was it really love that sent
you on that bloody, unrelenting trip?
Did sweet, daunting love have you in its grip
and make you dole out all that punishment?
While I suppose it must have played its part
I'll wager mulish honour and tradition
that doubled-headed yard dog of perdition
will have tugged far more sharply on your heart.
I guess you worked that out Don Corleone
on sad and splintered, cold Nevada nights
it wasn't love that swirled around your head
and sent you running terrified to Rome.
You knew before she said it Kay was right
that love, if held too tightly, turns to dread.

*Luke Wright*

## thou sHALt

////////////////////////////////
so much depends upon a bleached
white bone badged with brother's
blood beside the red embers thrown
who remembers the first ache to
kill? I do I'm the marrow within
your tomorrows your sin the mirror
to all men the yen the ken the end
of intelligence the camp fire at
night the stars' fires at night
the blind ire at night the hunger
and the hard-on the hard won the
far-gone the distant drawn near
the foregone wrong the hot breath
at the ear the click of tongues of
teeth that tickle flesh from bone
the swamp of home the summit of
being all godly alone the lure of
the infallible the sea of space
the mesh of maths the clearing
everyone from your path the lip-
synching of self my mind is going
to rack my mind is going to ruin
my mind is going to lullaby my
mind is going to rock you off
\\\\\\\\\\\\\\\\\\\\\\\\\\\\\\\\

*Simon Barraclough*

## Poem for Roy Batty

Whenever neon trickles down
to meet a city drain,
I think of you on some wet roof,
a cobbled son of men —

the thorned corona of your hair
that crowns a failing sun,
the closing lotus of your hand,
its nail to pin the flown;

and when the blue sky beckons through
a fissure in the rain,
you haunt the hurt leak of my pulse —
beat gone, beat gone, beat gone.

*Kona Macphee*

# Black Cloud Over My House Sometime In The 1960's

Look, that cloud
Black as Emma Peel's leather trousers
On our black and white television
In that front room with a canary in the corner. Emma,

Maybe trousers isn't the right word. Pants. Skin.
That cloud seems tight, full, tight. My voice
Is cracking at the edges

And there's a single hair on my chest
Like a wire or a spider's thigh.  I
Showed it to our John and he laughed.

Saturday night. Me and Emma, in the front room.
And our John. And my Dad. And my Mam.
And the canary, singing. And my single hair. And her trousers.

My dad joins me in the garden.
There'll be a cloudburst soon he says, his voice lilting.

*Ian McMillan*

## Avenger

Mum thought I'd love the trouser suit
she made me, but the only ones I'd seen
were on TV and at ten I didn't want
to set a local trend; following was safer.

The pattern showed a figure-hugging
outfit in black leather but mine was bulky,
scratchy wool, ill-fitting around my puppy fat.
If I'd had curves, it would have hidden them.

Still, the first time I wore it a boy wolf-whistled
and called me Cathy Gale.  I kicked him.

*Nancy Somerville*

## Max Wall

this poem
        refuses to have capitals on its top line / bonce
        it wears tight black vocabulary in patches
        neatly tailored and faintly shabby-chic
it has reverse-indented its lower quarters
    lifted by memory routines from before television
        including some of the movies, but has made celluloid
        molten, and drip-dried it off, and may come crack
    your teapot, on an obligatory home visit
in the name of fame
    for the weirdo
    I ally to

*Ira Lightman*

## And the doctor says *i.m. Tommy Cooper*

So he goes to the doctor
and the doctor says Haven't seen you for a while
and he says to the doctor Sorry, I've been ill

and the doctor says Stick your tongue out and stand by the window
and he says to the doctor Why?
and the doctor says I hate my neighbours

and the doctor says Say aaah
and he says to the doctor What for?
and the doctor says My dog is unwell

and he says to the doctor
I'm on a diet of whisky
and I've lost three weeks already

and he says to the doctor I used to drink it neat
but now I loosen my tie
and let my shirt flap from my trousers

and the doctor says You have to quit, your heart is weak
and he says to the doctor I want a second opinion
and the doctor says OK, you're ugly as well

and days later, only halfway through his set,
the doctor says He's D – E – A – D,
pronounced dead, and they had to close the

Oh what are they called?
those long drapey things that hang from a rail
Well, for him it was curtains

and then the crowd clapped
and then they howled out for more
and then they all stopped just like that

*Paul McGrane*

23

## Count Orlok

Mr Barlow in the film of *Salem's Lot*
had been bitten by this old and silent grandsire
– bloated tick of a head, and the white stare
daring its meal to blink; the spirit fingers
long, on arms themselves too long
for the ghost torso, ending in sickle
fingernails which reap around the edges.
That same affectless banshee gaze, as if
shocked to think what struggles in a sack;
the haunted arms retracted, sick with hunger's
tightening suck inside the drainpipe chest,
the stealth alive and jerky on the sudden
though oddly stiff, owing to his need
to put not a wraith foot wrong in this gloom
infested with the sicknesses of rats.
He was a phantom limb that ached between
Bram Stoker and Lugosi, the flickering amputation,
his awkwardly edited, overacted
jump cuts on Murnau's screen
killed by the light but repeatedly brought to life
through remembering projections. His stark skull
fathering the dome of Giger's Alien,
stared down all the gorgeous Hammer vampires.
And the teeth. His crowded cutters
not the canines of well bred familiars,
but front incisors for a rodent
piercing, sank themselves
into the undercurrent of our bloodstream,
decanting hidden dreams since '22
gorged on *Ulysses*, *The Waste Land*, *Nosferatu*.

*Jim Stewart*

# Report In Summary: Summerisle

Now the noughties, still on-duty,
Before long, that song! The birthday-
      Suited mare from upstairs began;
    I checked into The Green Man again.
I might've stayed, pulled up a pew
But fell for a honeyed ale to-go;
      It was beyond a man's control!
      That's when I saw him: Summerisle
Of seventy-three about the bay
Windowsill, with his lecherous way
      Of speaking, slurring drunk in a secular
      Age, but still in folk vernacular:
*"Would you have a wond'rous sight?*
*The midday sun at midnight!"*
      *Puts me in mind of a man whose lust*
      *Was burned up in the loch-land mist.*
*Time was, we men remained*
*Erect for longer, bein' made*
      *Of wicker, not of farmyard straw*
      *As we invariably nowadays are.*
*Look at us, Sergeant, at our ages*
*Waitin' for wakes of Nicholas Cages*
      *To scramble through the forecourt screamin'*
      *Bein' pursued by Crow, Drone, Queen:*
*Policeman, priest, straw man, strumpet!*
*Burn the wood, the cloth, the hood, the helmet!*
      Then in the sky, my siren again.
      Gosh, was that how long we'd been?
I had to dash. My phallic symbol
Threatened to rear its beery skull.
      I shan't arrest. The fields aren't ripe.
      I think we're finished. Stop the tape.

*Mark Burnhope*

## Tea with Derek and Clive

My bedroom door safe shut against family
the worn needle mines the dark groove
in the vinyl. Through the crackle, hiss
and spit Peter Cook is retrieving lobsters
from up Jayne Mansfield's bum. I imagine
it's one minute past closing time and he's drunk
(of course) so he wakes her up, what with the
nipping and all — *stop fucking nipping* — *Pete*
she says as he nips away nip nip nip
with the sugar tongs and the lobsters
aren't helping.  Downstairs my brother
is setting the table for tea, sharp knives
for tough meat, mum taps on the door.
Perhaps we can hear my LP while we eat,
she loves Peter Cook and Dudley Moore.

*Martin Figura*

## Dud

I never belittled him. Of course
he looked up to me, being himself
somewhat lacking in the leg division.
I had nothing against the other one.

Did I tell you, when he won
the organ scholar's gown
they had to take it up two feet?
Two feet, two feet, and only one of them right.

He followed me around, my chihuahua.
He clung like bloody Greta Garbo
until that business with tall blonde birds,
that sell-out Hollywood career.

Even when I'd departed
to my eternal basement club
he kept calling my answerphone,
dialling up on his piano.

The holy trampolining fool!
I was only pulling his leg.
I loved him too.
(But I can't talk now, because he's here).

*Anne Berkeley*

## Infamy

They have been at the dressing up box again
and are playing Romans in Egypt, mummies
and daddies, in Liz and Burton's cast off
frocks and togas. Cwor, indeed, Hengist.

This is glamour and fame or it's as close
as we'll get, but see, you can't be serious
even about the business of love and death
and Empires rise and fall and negligees

just fall and here comes the Empress. Quick,
Amanda Barrie, mine own angel of oop north,
in whose mouth asses butter wouldn't melt,
copyright now those Manga eyes, and yours

might be salvation. No, love and death come
momentarily to us all. Some of this is true.
Sid's a thuggish goat, Hawtrey a mincing lush
and yes Kenny, they have got it in for you.

*Tim Turnbull*

# Carry On Chopping

Plenty of slicing going on and from blade to neck
laughter all the way, but thanks for your concern.
The beheaded are French aristocrats, the executioner
Kenneth Williams, and Sid the Black Fingernail raises
fingers to revolution from his stately home in Surrey.
A subplot in themselves, Joan Sims directs her breasts.
Kenneth freaks out when a hirsute man he imagined
a woman kisses him – twice! – but reasserts his sex
by unsheathing a sword. By now the Fingernail rides
through France searching for the lovely Jacqueline,
bearer of his mother's denture necklace. Love is blind,
immediate and tasteless, and gives hope to us all.
Robespierre is tied-up, literally. Jacqueline reveals
unexpected flair for the harp. If it's hard to follow
the non-sequiturs, a door explodes to blow your mind
elsewhere while the Fingernail catapults through
Joan's windowpane and makes promises he never
intends to keep. We penetrate the movie's moral heart.
Kenneth unsheathes – twice! in one film – but the latest
craze is for bulletholes in wallpaper. "Don't shoot!
Mind the furniture! Use your swords!" Kenneth howls.
A plate shatters. "This would never have happened
before the revolution!" Snail-brained Bidet swings
an axe and revolutionary pillars collapse beneath
an avoirdupois of narrative. A double guillotine rewards
Kenneth, lying side-by-side with the trusty Bidet
like undercooked lamb chops at a postmodern barbecue,
possibly the most liberating moment of his life.

*Rob A MacKenzie*

## Orange

I have the wet of an orange
on my tongue, my chin, a rime
of pith beneath my fingernails.
My head's filled with the insistent chime
of guitars singing the sea's rush.
In the front room, adverts roll and fade
like the tide, or a remembered kiss.
How easily and wrongly I am swayed.
I hold another pitted globe up to the light.
Oh yes, the future. The future's bright.

*Adam Horovitz*

## Unsure

My body stinks
on my second day of camping wild,
my first morning in his bed;
and then today,
when the radiographer
clamps my breast against the metal plate
and tilts my head,
so that I breathe the hemmed-in, sour-grass odour of my oxter
and will myself to smell well,
to get out of here with a great big tick on my back.

*Alison Grant*

## Flake

Not the woman lying in the bath,
steam rising as her toes curl round the taps
and not the way she holds the melting flake
poised between her mouth and fingertips
as the hot water rises, overflows the rim
while she dreams on oblivious
but the moment just before she sighs,
brushing a crumb of chocolate from her lips.

*Ian Parks*

## Halifax

No longer from Halifax, no longer a bank,
but a notional music radio station,
peopled with people who find things funny
that are not funny, who find things great
that are not great, who find things fun
that are not fun, who would be first
against the wall when the revolution comes,
if it hadn't already come, and gone.

*Nick Asbury*

## Lego

How come, when all their customers
inhabit a green-field paradise,
does my bank branch in town
resemble a cardboard kingdom
of percentages – the manager
a no-sayer, glum as any Calvinist,
and not a red Lego brick in sight ?

*Vivien Jones*

# Rogue

See into its black doll's eyes, see through them too:
the murky garden, sandbed, waving weed, it muscles through.

No volunteers, no mates. Takes one to know one.
Slow fingernail, nerve-filleting, announcing you

have got the measure of this bird, this island –
too many captains here. Out there, bad fish.

The can-crunch idiom, that finny peak, gun-metal grey,
and eyes of washed-out blue. A nautical cliché,

Master of Orca. In spite of yourself, you got yourself
some tender-handed crew: three men in a boat

comparing scars, cracking jokes;  scored limbs, that broken
heart, the One That Got Away. Drink to your legs,

to Amity.  Sing Farewell and Adieu, as the whales join in.
Wiggle your jaggy tooth and grin, that party trick.

And the tattoos, that tattoo you wish the salt
had burned clean through, deceiving emblem.

Etched so long, a tale fades to an outline;
terror's made of darker ink.  But actions speak.

And thank you Mr Quint, you've been taken under
advisement.  A little shaking, a little tenderising,

and down you go. The head, the tail, the whole damned thing.
Our shark. You'll never put on a lifejacket again.

*Isobel Dixon*

# The last of the little green men

From words of Shakespeare much knowledge
can be gained. Difficult to see the future is,
but these plays often insights contain.
The rise of the Dark Side consider: Lear
and Hamlet fine parallels provide.
Encroaching blindness, dying, a poisonous madness,
betimes recall the wit of Solo and Lord Vader's rage.
Descent and resurrection, all Campbell's themes,
loss of the mother, jealousy of the father,
discovery of the unknown Other,
all archetypal are.

I too an archetype am.
How many the Mekon remember?
My green nest-mate, long retired,
over his cloned Treen army hovered
on an inverted iron, war on Venus directing.
Defeat by Dan Dare, Skywalker's ancestor,
inevitable was. Good over evil
triumphs always. My words mark.

Back to my egg return I shall,
to the nest wherein was I laid.
Whence we came, thereto shall we all
back go. Time backwards runs.
Lost labour's love, Caesar Julius,
all Dreams of night's midsummer,
upon the stage their hour fret
and strut. A walking shadow
life is. More no.

*Colin Will*

## It's not all Alastair Sim, you know

I'm going to tell you about Ealing. Not the Ealing you know so well,
It's not all Alastair Sim, you know, drawled in a lilting smirk,
crawling with armchair secrets secreted by cool, wired, eccentrics.
I'm going to tell you about Ealing when films were forged in back gardens
and in simple greenhouses primed to catch as much sun as can be caught
while coughing up an unappetising pea soup. Fresh air was best
west of town. Bill Barker came from the east, carrying cameras,
supporting kids, wife, mother, brother. Bald, a small man, he shouts
in slang through megaphone at actors, extras, hands, hangs around
Her Majesty's stage door and picks up Sir Herbert's mob of luvvies.
The sleepy actors yawn in bright, unfamiliar morning, bump
and knock against each other in hackney cabs, roll towards the sunset
to get Tree's version of *Henry VIII*, such a hit with the carriage trade,
immortalised on celluloid in a single day, fixing a feature worthy to open
the new picture palaces thrown up in mass fit of civic pride bursting out
in Blackley, Teesside, Aberdeen. Yet all prints are burned six weeks
after the first screening — a gross publicity stunt. Ink cartoons Barker,
sleeves rolled up, as a workman shovelling nitrate into a fireplace
while his actor-manager buddy flings his velvet-draped arm to protest
this outrageous travesty. But Barker and Tree are in cahoots,
and fed by this fertiliser the studio blooms. Pressure of orders mounts,
the fortunes of Ealing are founded. So one day, creepy Alastair Sim will entice
us, credulous, into the old glass house, gently lifting his heavy eyelids:
*Come in me dears, and feel the bitter soul of the miser hurt and heal.*

*Jude Cowan*

## why we dance

imagine, every time we went to kiss
we stopped    spittle-length apart
holding the tensed-bow of our lips
and looked at each other

                                        (film demands close-up)

and that the looking dug an empty shelf between us
and imagine we thought that if we memorised enough
from the fabric of each other's skin that we might
lay such small facts down and walk across them to each other

but that the distance was great    and each attempt to touch
tore the seam at our feet a little wider
and imagine we tried so often
that we accumulated millions of these small facts

until they were too many and too much
like a length of cloth which can't be folded tight enough to store
and that the only other thing we knew to do was dance
and that the dancing didn't bring us closer

but at least we were doing the same thing    at the same time
and that all our facts unspooled and blew around our legs
and imagine our backs, arching in colour    our impossible hands

*Andrew McMillan*

# M

Like 'The story of O',
blurring power and submission,
M seeks to control
Bond's rampant ambition.
Her suits unremarkable,
name not revealed…
Matriarch or Madonna?
MI6 lips are sealed.

She chastises James,
'Relic of the cold war,
you're a sexist,
misogynist dinosaur!'
Her judgement can end him,
but she admires his defiance,
indulging his ego
and lack of compliance.

Bond's boss, not Bond-girl,
with bikini-fit brain;
succumbing to charm
muscular yet urbane.
They spar like prize fighters
whenever they meet,
over unfinished business
and deaths indiscreet.

M partners a whisky,
shoots an iced stare;
brow cocked in a challenge
for this Double Dare.
Bond kindles her power,
seeks her permission…
a willing accomplice,
he feigns his submission.

*Charlie Jordan*

## Q Advises 007 On Affairs Of The Heart

I recommend you keep yourself concealed
and do not give your purposes away
It could be useful to you in the field

The plans should be hermetically sealed,
the combination coded to your DNA
I recommend you keep yourself concealed

Never let them see behind your shield —
offer them a cigarette and bingo! I daresay
it could be useful to you in the field

A smaller weapon's easier to wield,
and you can always trust your Walther PPK
I recommend you keep yourself concealed

If your cover's blown and you're revealed
there's always the ejector seat to save the day
It could be useful to you in the field

The technical details are in the dossier
Apart from that, there's nothing more to say
I recommend you keep yourself concealed
It could be useful to you in the field

*Alan Smithee*

# Smiley

All these words, all these elaborate
names for episodes in which someone
we thought we liked turns out not to like us,
or someone dies, we eat lunch and feel
that something has changed, but things
go on precisely as before: when I lie awake
it's to think up the clever phrases
we will use, later, between ourselves,
to refer to our failures. It's a kind of game.

I have the cunning of a virgin and Satan's
proud, misfiring, ineffective conscience.
The skill is to quietly eat a meal and listen
to someone you despise let slip
the blabs of pause and intonation
that turn the continents in your mind.
I run a hand over my thinning hair.
I'm really very good indeed. I was.

I'm suspicious of flower-sellers,
of the gossip column, of beef pies.
Sometimes I fall asleep and dream
and in the dream I fall asleep and dream
I'm playing chess, and then I wake up
and my wife has left me. I'm working
on some translations of Racine...
for my own amusement... Did I really
not leave my hat? Well, perhaps
it's in the taxi. Thank you again. Good night.
These aren't the droids you're looking for.

*Tony Williams*

## Classified

Insubordinate Sergeant Palmer,
blinking blondly: what a charmer.

Searchlight spectacles, off just for bed,
reads your field reports by cocking his head.

But Harry's file's not in the tray;
Even his Zodiac's gone astray.

Another scam? Bird on expenses?
Clerical error, Ministry of Defence's?

*Mozart and champignons, one-fifty a year?*
*He's legged it to Berlin for some bitte beer.*

*A British warrant officer would never leave his lighter,*
*let alone official secrets, with some Russian blighter.*

*Isn't there some rule that all our moles*
*should at least hold a Fellowship at All Souls?*

When the bandstand's quiet and the cold war's done
He'll send us a postcard to tell us who won.

Has he really defected? An ugly rumour,
but I shall miss that sense of humour.

*Patrick Andrews*

## Bruce Lee

My father watched Bruce Lee when he was drunk.
He'd rewind, play, rewind the same fight scenes:
the Colosseum, cat's-hiss, snapping neck;
the crack of mirrors, endless halls of glass

he'd rewind, play, rewind; the same fight scenes
for boyfriends, or our friends, or just for us.
The crack of mirrors, endless halls of glass.
*Just watch this scene!* It was a kind of test

for boyfriends, or our friends, or just for us:
the fists, the kick and Bruce's blood-striped chest.
*Just watch this scene!* It was a kind of test.
We knew that Bruce, by 32, was dead,

the fists, the kick and Bruce's blood-striped chest.
My father needed heroes to exist.
We knew that Bruce, by 32, was dead,
but good won out: again, again, it did.

My father needed heroes to exist,
the Colosseum, cat's-hiss, snapping neck.
But good won out: again, again, it did.
My father watched Bruce Lee when he was drunk.

*Clare Pollard*

# Three Rounds to K.O. Joe Pesci

*Don't get scared now,* the kid said
but man, I was. Micro Machines!
Any real McCallister couple would've spread
a traffic cop stinger-strip for him
instead of the red carpet they did
at the Grammys. All of those filming days
spent covered in chicken feathers,
steam-iron stamps on the forehead,
Stars of David in both feet, where
all his Christmas paraphernalia cut in my skin.

Kickin' back with badfellas in big-gun bars,
casinos, just to fuckin' amuse you! Okay,
so I worked around a riff, said something:
Go fuck ya mother's what I said, right,
which was neither funny nor articulate but,
like time, was money. How was I funny?
Gassing around resting, walking parks
and beaches, bathed in the bleeding light
of a thumping-heart, boxing-glove lamp?
I had to inhabit a man who lived like that.

Here, portraying the brother
of middle-weight boxer, Jake La Motta:
Now playing in black and white, me and De Niro
about to punch each other out:
'What does it prove?
What does it prove?
What does it prove?'
over and over. Close your eyes
for one single gasp-for-breath second: your raging
bullshitter's boxing title, mobster dragster, cop car.

*Mark Burnhope*

## Mouse

*He doesn't know his strength.* It's comical.
You wake up in an arch of daylight feeling that
your head's been clobbered with a frying pan,
your hand clamped in a red-hot waffle iron,
your ear nailed jocularly to the picket fence.

*He can't help himself.* You only wanted cheese,
a taste of cream, a cherry as big as your head:
a rest. Eyes wide at the plenty of his table
you tucked the napkin underneath your grin,
lifted up a luck-bright knife to carve the turkey –

*My own fault; clumsy.* Then the panting chase
from yard to kennel, the slow-motion dash,
the usual dynamite. The kitchen-table stagger,
hammer, broom and slapstick fall; those
lively punishments, those stars and little birds.

Every day you mean to pack your nightcap,
take up your crumbs and banjo, march off
in a swanee whistle fanfare. Above the hole
where home used to be you'll nail a slapdash sign –
*That's all, folks.*

*Jo Bell*

42

## Dastardly and Muttley

*Wake up Muttley, you're dreaming again*
*you're not Robin Hood and you're not Gunga Din*
*you're not a brave knight or a king who's been crowned*
*you're just plain old Muttley, the sniggering hound.*
Wake up Dick, you're dreaming again,
You're not Terry Thomas, you are not Jack Lemmon.
Your races are canned, no intent to re-master,
you're just plain old Dick, the sad losing Dastard.

Face facts Dick, your pigeon has flown,
Penelope Pitstop's a withered old crone,
Muttley's banged-up in some celluloid pound,
word on the street's he's not sniggering now.
Too bad, Dick, moustaches are out,
Great Danes and grunge became what it's about.
Your mean machine doesn't mean squat in 2D;
your life's beyond enhancing digitally.

Hard luck Dick, you gave it your best
but Hanna-Barbera has laid you to rest
your sky-written CGI epitaph reads
*sassafrassruckedover Rick Rastardly.*

*Heather Reid*

# Here

It's a small town, land-locked, the kind of place
you adore as a kid, trawling its further limits:
the hill that forms its northern border,
the river hemming its outskirts; the warp
and weft of its humdrum streets etched
on your mind from the days you rose at six
to deliver the local news.

By fourteen a place you only want to leave,
hours spent in your bedroom embroidering
your escape into anonymity, adventure, a future.
And for a few short years you make it;
spinning like a shuttle through its outer orbit,
you dazzle and delight from afar.

But then you meet a small-town girl, get hitched,
and before you know it you're back,
a baby on the way, tithed to the building society,
setting up a small business or learning the ropes
at the family firm; the relatives en masse round
your Mum's every Sunday, a post on the PTA,

the teachers who taught you now teaching your kids,
wondering how on earth you wound up here
instead of elsewhere.

*Patricia Ace*

# Two Tales of Brigadoon

*In 2011, a Vegas tycoon left $4 million to the National Trust for Scotland before committing suicide. Although he had never visited Scotland he had loved his fantasies of a long vanished land. His mythical Scotland was most famously portrayed in 'Brigadoon' where the American traveller, Tommy, meets and falls in love with the mysterious Fiona.*

Far better if he'd bade farewell forever and returned
to his American bitch, her withering elegance, the bars
all mirrors and champagne, each gold bubble far more
substantial than Brigadoon. She was a dream of foaming
primrose skirts, dancing foot perfect through forests
of white heather but memory would have taken care
of her. Far better these New York streets with their
chipped stone exteriors and drenched with weather
than the phantom country which rose from the mists
once every blessed century, removed from history.
Only the arching bridge seemed real, stone on stone.
He turned his back on the village and crossed back over.

Mid-century, he retired to the gritty glare of the Vegas desert,
a recluse who'd shaken hands with Eisenhower. Fifty years
later he wrote his will in a firm determined hand leaving
millions to the memory of bonnie lassies who breathed
like rain-soaked breezes only in the soundstage of his mind.
Then he fired a bullet through his skull and the scenery cracked.
Did he leave with the illusion that his dark journey would
carry him over desert, cities, a chilly ocean, or had he
accepted that night cannot deftly shape the welcoming
silhouettes of inns and houses, spark them into life and light.
The stars are clearer in the desert than almost anywhere.
In his fine house he lies. His heart still bleeds for her.

*Tracey Herd*

## Violation

It isn't the swagger, staccato jargon, the smirk or spark
in your eyes. You don't know subtlety and that's a turn on to me.

It isn't even the snug fit of your chartreuse tunic, smoking hot with
phaser burns and blood, your pudgy love handles sucked in for all they
are worth.

I've pleasured Romulans, clung on to the ribbed domes of Klingons but
no male in the known universe has ever made man bags look quite so
gallant.

It's not the gravitas of your middle name, recalling a Caesar, or how you
pull off a wreath of leaves for your caramel head to crown a short-skirted
toga.

A cheeky glimpse of your gleaming chest and lickable nipples yearning
through the slash of velour, your bulging pecs make my insides ripple.

The hard decisions you make in an instant and the way your chin-jutting
masculinity probes into existence wherever you choose set my phasers
humming.

But when you don that gold bolero, the sash tied just so at your hip, you
buckle
your swash with such élan and sell me the lie that we make a lovely
couple.

Beam me up, warp my drive Tiberius, let me peel your grapes one by
one. Violate
my Prime Directive, who cares about logic? Yours forever, a little slave
girl from Orion.

Besides, once you go green, you'll always be keen.

*Dzifa Benson*

## Picard: A Promotional Postcard

Jean-Luc. Oh look at you all ceremonial
gold braided, captain's four stars winking
on your collar, Federation badge bold
on your heart, a miniature *Enterprise,* cut
it seems from a sliver of moonstone, which
planet's moon of course impossible to tell,
your dress whites padded and pointed
just ready for that deft little tug of *make it so,*
THAT voice echoing basso-profundo on the bridge
via Stratford's stage. Could you be any sexier?
Not a wink, not a flicker of expression, part
of the effect. How else would we know
we were in safe hands? Not just our weekly
assignation on your bridge — that was a given.
You never let me down, not even with Romulans
to out-manoeuvre...Weren't they the ones with the cool
*bird of prey* ships who could *cloak themselves* at will?
Every Tuesday, there you were, at a flick of a switch
courtesy of our new cable set-up. My teenage son
and me. I think he thought he was Wesley Crusher,
all big brown awe-struck sulky eyes, unable to walk
down the street with me, but happy enough to
*boldly go.* Me, him and you. (A new generation indeed
and certainly neither of us could stand that sludgy-mustard
tunic-ed lot who creakily came before!) His gift the Rumi poems
*Happy Christmas Mum! Hope you like the bookmark!*
And here you are, still, marking a place in a poem
*At night you're my deepest sleep...But could we be together*
*outside of time as well as inside?* Could not have put it better.
We still have time. You could play your flute.
I'll read Rumi to you. Ah. The Beloved.

*Sheila Templeton*

47

## Taste the Blood of Dracula

Dark blue crombie,
black velvet collar,
screaming scarlet socks.
To the night from the night.

To the night from the night;
stepping from our houses –
starlings darting si lent ly to flock –
wrapped in the city, a doleful grey.
If asked the shade, I'd say boredom.

Dracula on the telly,
reggae on the stereo,
trouble on the terraces:
we were the horrors.

Stepping from our houses,
aggro falling drun ken ly our way.
With fangs poised,
knuckles and brogues
delightfully blooded.

*Tim Wells*

# McGuffin's Tune

1.
You whistle it cheerily. It is an ordinary morning,
Just as the crop-spraying plane swoops menacingly low
Or the train enters the tunnel, as gathering birds grow
Unpleasantly intrusive, as the desperate warning

Phone call sets you off across an alien landscape.
What is it called? Where's memory when you need
To discover elemental truth? Notes bleed
Through your ear as you are plotting your escape.

And then a statuesque blonde woman with hair
Like a fortress appears at the corner of your eye
And the whole world tips into chaos. Uncertain

Of your role in this, you contemplate an affair
That ends in horror. What is the tune? And why
Whistle it now, just there, by the shower curtain?

2.
McGuffin is the empty box on the baggage rack.
McGuffin is the nothing that makes your fortune.
McGuffin is the alternative name for the tune
You are whistling as shadows shift at your back.

*McGuffin the name. So terribly pleased to meet you.*
But are you the true McGuffin, the real McCoy?
Is McGuffin a man or an ingenious toy
Whose function is to unmask you then beat you?

Whistle the tune and keep on whistling, it is
What everybody does in the dark after all.
The first four bars are simple but the next

Four you've forgotten. You chase them through cities
Of guilt and hurt until you hear them call
Like death itself: clear, serious, perplexed.

*George Szirtes*

# The Blue And The Green

Now here's a funny thing –
I come home last night to find the missus
in her curlers, holding up a green book
in one hand, a blue book in the other.

She said she didn't mind the book with tales
of pretty girls on bikes who go to church,
and milkmen, full of whimsy, on their rounds,
fresh from hands of rummy with sweet Mary

from the dairy. But ruddy hell! This other one,
its pages falling open at the chapter
where it tells of honeymooners in hotels
their hands below the dinner table,

while upstairs a tidy little chambermaid
is cornered by the big-boned concierge
while bending down to dust the skirting.
Here's a chap who takes his little Brownie out,

and snaps away at washing lines weighed down
with stays and corsets swinging in the breeze, while
blowsy land girls wink. All clever stuff, no rubbish,
like the feller who cleans out his rabbits while

his wife looks from the step and dreams of Dick,
the sly commercial traveller who calls in
every week while her old man's on nights to get his
pinstripes pressed and shine her warming pan.

*Who writes this filth?* she says, her housecoat
quivering. *It just ain't fit for decent folk.*
*So give it back* I says. *Not on your life* she says
*I still got fifty pages more to read.*

*Andy Jackson*

50

# Singing Happiness

"How tickled I am!" we laughed, walking to the car,
carrying  out remnants of a *Knotty-Ash-jam-butty* picnic,

excited from our marathon of laughing,
fingers rubbing aching tummies.  What a show!

How dad had grinned when I asked the auditorium,
"Mum, have you seen his tickling stick? It's huge!"

Gently, her voice sang to twin tub and to mangle.
Gleefully, she tickled out cobwebs.  Softly, seductively, she sang,

angling rainbow feathers, chasing us through the living room.
"Ooh, Mum… enough!" we cried, "we submit! We submit!"

"It's important," she'd urge me in quiet moments."… education!
Shouldn't waste your brain… clever girl… don't waste the hours."

'Ours' was a happy home until, blessed by Trojan gifted education,
shunning the abstract noun, playing a game of show not tell;

elegies  were all my moleskin notebooks would allow. *Happiness,
essentially,* scholars say, *is written white; served in clichés; often trite.*

I trust they may, in ivory towers, be right but on our council house estate,
state what you like, it did us all the power of good to hear my mother
sing.

*Julie Boden*

51

## The Child Catcher Child

I was eleven
when my gift was revealed
in a game of hide and seek.

After that, word got around
and I was not allowed to join in
except once, when they tied me to a tree.

A fleshy boy held out a woodcut
of Hansel and Gretel
as they all skipped around me.

I'd uncovered every child,
and winkled out those
who didn't know they were hiding

behind curtains, in glory holes,
in the church yard, in attic rooms;
the smell of pork cooked in honey and milk.

*Helen Ivory*

## Merciless

Resurrected again, the Emperor Ming
      falls into the highly eccentric orbit
            of the satellite TV talk-show circuit.

A merciless wit and non-stop raconteur,
      Ming proves that, at the end of the day,
            villains really do get all the best lines.

"Take my wife," he says, "be my guest —
      I used detonation synthesis to make this
            diamond from my consort's mortal remains."

Charming his hosts and studio audiences,
      and dazzling millions of viewers at home,
            the tyrant who ruled a world becomes a star.

But his conquest of the small screen
      still leaves something to be desired:
            his ultimate victory has been all too easy.

He misses Gordon, his corn-fed nemesis —
      now long gone and all but forgotten —
            the tow-headed yang to his obsidian yin.

Ming takes time out from his busy schedule,
      steals DNA from Flash and Dale's joint grave,
            and creates the child they should have had.

She makes her debut on *The Late Late Show*,
      only seven years old and already a spitfire:
            "That's my girl," he says, "make me proud."

*Andrew J. Wilson*

## Poem for the Maudlin End Titles of *The Sweeney*

"The stars are up there, George,
but we rarely get a chance
to lift our heads long enough
to see the buggers."

The lads stroll through Soho,
the 'papers scream corruption,
the scrubbers just scream.

They're hard hours, the ones between pubs.
Jack, face the colour of a cheap envelope,
checks his watch,

forces all his life's experience
into conscious thought:
"Somebody put something in my drink...
alcohol."

*Tim Wells*

# Callan

*Title Sequence*
A lightbulb sweeping letters on a redbrick wall spells out his name,
bites the bullet with its filament : a halogen Osram going ballistic.

*Scene 1*
A warehouse (a disused Z-Cars set). Callan in a sheepskin, Toby
in a trenchcoat. A villain in an Anglia. Screeching tyres. A gun fires.

*Scene 2*
As scene 1, minus the warehouse, the car and any further action,
apart from changing the blinking lightbulb.

*Voices off*
*Mr. Callan! Mr. Callan! Come quickly, Mr. Callan!*

*Exposition*
Episodes austere as sodium is to neon's opulence imploded in
claustrophobic studios, were sectioned to the vaults, canned
and mothballed. A Hunter, a Valentine, a Porter and a Mower
played the minor parts while Woodward went from Wicker Man
to wicker chair. Brutal nights with government thugs and angsty
assassins flew swifter than the Sweeney cars or Lonely fivers
on rank outsiders. Few can summon this character — no Kojak,
Kuryakin or Corleone — but dully British in a series dimly recalled
as 40 watts of bleakness swinging on a twisted cord: Logie Baird
goading Edison into suicide.

*Commercial Interlude*
And now for a few words from our sponsors —
*Marlboro Lights Cigarettes.* (Give you lungs like string vests)
*Nothing sucks like Electrolux.* (Apart from swingeing council cuts)
And another bullet in the guts for the Osram —
*Mazda lamps stay brighter longer, always ask for Mazda!*

*Eddie Gibbons*

## Doctor Love

Doctor, Doctor, when you first called I was nine.
I couldn't come with you then, still hiding behind daddy,
sheltering in his shadow in front of our monochrome set
dreaming of Gallifrey, of diving into your kaleidoscope.

I was changing like you, renewing all my cells,
going through to my third incarnation:
a new version of myself with pointed breasts, long hair,
a waist. Not nylon slacks but Levi's, lace and scent.

Doctor, Doctor, oh you dandy, velvet smoking jacket,
bow ties and leather gloves, you lounge lizard.
My mother warned me about men like you.
And yet you were the perfect gentleman, like daddy.

I watched as you outfaced Silurians, always polite
but not afraid to punch when words failed,
reverse the polarity and get the hell out of there.
I was getting out too: boys, A levels, university.

Doctor, Doctor, your world was colour like mine.
We watched you in black and white but knowing
others could see your green, burgundy and blue
as you strutted in galaxies, finding yourself, like me.

Daddy's girl learned to argue, teenstruck and difficult.
I had no TARDIS to travel back to myself. You
could have made everything alright again.
Where were you? Too busy on missions to call again.

Doctor, Doctor, you missed your chance with me.

*Angela Topping*

## Who Knew

*"People are quite happy believing the wrong things."* Tom Baker

Seen first on the floor of UNIT prone, a miasma
of black and white, that smile not yet in evidence
as the credits rolled, his new form firmed up.

Regeneration absolute, the smile filled up a screen
where interference passed for SFX, jelly babies
were a metaphor for nothing worse than glee.

That scarf too, only some mad simile for DNA,
and topped by floppy curls that any latent hippy
would've died for – if they'd spoken like that then.

The Doctor couldn't do it, couldn't die, grappled
every cliff-hanger and grinned them out unfazed:
no plastic alien, cardboard spaceship ever up to him.

What was he on, we wondered, seriously stoned,
as the 70s progressed unchecked? That lit-up smile
betokened more than on-another-planet, man.

Out of the box? No way. The TARDIS flew him
off through time and space, dimensions relative
to those we tracked him by – the box we turned on

weekly, watched flicker in a moment back to life.

*Brian Johnstone*

## Massage

A thing of beauty is a joy for ever,
with a slick of stay-put shine!
Because image is everything. Imagine
passing into nothingness.
Because mirrors won't crack,
but hearts will. Hand-made
by robots. Because
you're worth it.

*Tiffany Anne Tondut*


## Specsavers

Clouds hum across the metal sky and lines of wind are scrawled
across the air as I listen to the radio telling me to stay indoors
or if I have to go out at least take an umbrella or a crash helmet.
Rain crawls over scabby hills and sheep are walking to my door.
They're coming to say I've let myself go, complain about haircuts,
to say they feel like hell, demand food, shelter from the lashes
from the Atlantic and it's time that they discussed pension plans.

*Rodney Wood*


## Five-a-Day

The advert air-brushed broccoli
in such a glowing way
I vowed it would become a part
of all our Five-a-Day.

I swore that what I'd bought this time
would not be left to waste —
until I found they hadn't tried
to air-brush out its taste.

*Martin Parker*

## Milky Bar Kid

*Here comes the Milky Bar Kid*
Smart ass swinging on a wire fence
between two barbs.
I laughed, the laugh of a betrayer.
My brother,
red blush against white hair,
small glasses magnifying the ground,
*The Milky Bars Are On Me*
ripples after him,
in taunting, bitter chocolate.

*Nicola Marshall*


## Meerkat

Tripod tails A-lined to balance
out bi-pedal curiosity
paws poised (tommy-cooperish)
bright-eyed interrogatory
looks to camera—simple
blood-and-sand realities twist
toward cute as families
of charismatic megafauna
socialize (infant-killers cannibals)—
and me, I flip to channel three
where meerkats merely milk
celebrity to sell insurance.

*Jude Marr*

## Louise Brooks

Pearls strung around a neck
of marble, lustrous beads
hard and pretty: the hair is black,
the lips rubescent. Ghost men feed

on these painted curves, define
a role you played with vigour, silent
vigour. The eyes are cool and sane.
The mood is violent.

*Tracey Herd*

## Promises, Promises

*To Jayne Mansfield*

You started strong — a *publicity whore*,
they said, who would do anything to score
a front page spread. You'd brave it — show some skin
for any shutterbug, a not-quite-Marilyn
who worked the bad boy's dream, that perfect slut
whose celluloid extremes were never cut,
a naked first. What's left to emulate?
Those sad initials rusting on a gate
on Sunset Boulevard, rushes of breasts —
your racked up offerings that urged and pressed
like gorgeous, curdled gifts forced behind lace
and bone. They never seemed to know their place.
Overworked, over-exposed, on the make,
they spilled like cream take after take after take.

*Jacqueline Saphra*

## Stalag Luft III

Was the prison camp in The Great Escape
Seventy-six men made it out through the tunnel
But it's all very arthouse if we don't care about
One

And I do
But not the one who commands the screen
Hollywood moto-punk Steve McQueen
No, I seek my hero among the many
And I find him. Angus Lennie

The little Scots bloke who dug the tunnel
But when his turn came wouldn't, couldn't try for freedom
Broke down underground havering in his actor's arch tones
About nights out in Hamilton before the war (he'd been a jockey),
Musselburgh, Ayr

And he taught us the trick of being grateful curled toes despite
That the camera was rolling and the lights were on us
And although our token countryman crumbled in clammy cowardice
At least they allowed us a speaking part at all

Angus had previous - Sunny Jim in Para Handy
Lovingly fleshed MacMawkish roles crowd out his grim c.v.
And subsequent too
To the shame of all Lennies
In the Crossroads Motel he was Shughie McFee

A part of such cringeable cod-Jock frippery
I grue at a distance of thirty-odd years
Camp as ... well ... as Stalag Luft III, I suppose
McFee used to make me want to take two showers

But our man got his moment as "The Mole" in The Great Escape
Yes, they stifled the life of him and us all into their script
Then the cameras rolled and the lights were on Angus
And he got to say his words but he did not break for freedom

*Robin Cairns*

62

## Shawshank Survivor

Into this stench of fear and piss,
the guilty come: only bars divide.
Screws and convicts both the same.
They read what's written on the walls
and in men's eyes.

There are so many ways to leave.
Be kicked to death on your first night,
serve forty years before parole
spits you out like phlegm back to
a world you cannot recognise.

To save one man, an unseen cloak:
his human pride, and sense to make
the best of things, to keep inside
the spark of hope, the grain of truth
the skill that others only lack.

His cell a planetful of thoughts:
the library stock a freedom march,
his chess set carved from rocks a game of war,
the wall behind a pin-up girl a hole in time.
He changes tack

knows law for what it is, a fake,
and sets about the life he wants to make.
An aria to feed their minds, to fill
the tawdry air with soaring joy,
to cock a snook at warden crook,
a plan of years to gain his prize:
a beach, a boat, the sun upon his back.

*Angela Topping*

## Taking Dorothy

It's not so long till dawn, but the clock is unmoving.
The ticket of a minute prints shadow on the bed.
Morning queues at the blinds, light admitted in strands.

Judy knows better than to clutch at its straws, retraces
her steps to the bathroom, a slow walk towards knowing
who will appear there, with her basket of half-baked hope.

Dorothy breaks in to the half-way house between night
and day, always, worn by her hike back from Oz. Pigtails
gnawed rope, soles of feet encrusted in her own blood;

It's ruby slipper there's just no taking off. Wired,
the actress, ready for ambush, to tear off the mask
the girl wears of her face, crumple it into her mouth.

No, Judy admits it, she was never a friend to Dorothy,
coming back to eye her like Lassie when wrestled to ground,
elastic binding her chest shredded, shiny tin heart exposed.

In the jaundiced en-suite Judy waits for a sketch of blue/white
to appear in the mirror. Once more, Dorothy will wave up
from its murky pond. Tonight only, the woman swears

she won't let the girl drown; she will take her hand in her own
and lead her down a road that goes somewhere towards home.

*Angela Readman*

# No Sound of Music?

Say she'd slept in for her very first audition, missed the bus, caught flu.
Fox might have made the film with someone else or maybe not at all
(like Paramount) but either way, there's total no recall. Did anyone
climb every mountain? Or march in rings around that fountain? Who

in a hopeful 'sixties childhood learned to sing about the edelweiss,
edelweiss, or heard the lonely goat-herd yodel to a female deer. Doe?
No sixteen going on anything for us, no summer house, no ray
of golden sun. We never got to catalogue – My favourite things: a few.

We were eight and going on nine, ready to collect those big screen
moments
like the Beatles cards we'd hoarded earlier which live on dog-eared,
chewed by memory. So Ringo still but no Maria, nor dressed in sailor
suits
and summoned by the Captain's whistle, Liesl, Kurt, Friedrich and crew.

No dresses out of curtains, no guitar. No Max, no nasty Baroness – a
villain
we could almost hiss at. Mary Poppins? Nah, not close and no cigar. We
missed
the geography of hills alive, the songs and history, the crowd's applause
as spotlights focused on a middle-of-the-night escape (which wasn't even
true).

Pitch perfect, yes, but no rose named for her. What poise, what
confidence
we might have learned. Instead no need without excuse to sing-a-long on
cue.
It might have done something good but bid auf wiedersehen to that.
Goodbye.
No Oscars (five), no digital repeats. Just heave a sigh. Forget that last
adieu. Adieu.

*Eleanor Livingstone*

# Walmington-on-Sea

Those monochrome Cold War years
of endless strikes, collapsing governments;
oil crises, power cuts, three-day weeks.
Walmington, your *on-Sea* largely taken
on trust: how gladly we fell into the womb
of your church hall, with its ineffectual
vicar, parade ground for Mainwaring's men.
*Mainwaring* – his very name betrayed
a postured life, lower-middle-class bluff
and bluster concealing the panic within;
a barrage balloon, deflated every episode
by Wilson's arched eyebrow, his *mot juste* –
this was the old England, where each man
must know his place. A pre-nuclear Eden,
the enemy disarmed by their own comedy
accents – *Your name vill also go on ze list.*
*Vott is it?* Don't tell him, Pike; mock him
with your playground rhymes, then wrap up
warm in the scarf your mother knitted you.
Join your comrades, marching in a sunlit
wood as the credits roll, a procession
fixed as a mummers' play: each week
Jones will stumble, Frazer will stare
with his wild, wild eyes, Walker will draw
on a crafty fag; and Godfrey will smile
his beneficent, baby-faced smile.
Walmington: the length of time, from now
to when I saw you first, is more than the span
from then to the war itself. It is a double
refraction, a novelty paperweight held
inside a novelty paperweight. Let me shake
the hemispheres, conjure their knowable
weather; then lose myself in the crazy
swirl of imitation snow.

*Alan Buckley*

## Barmaids

Let's all salute the barmaids of the Rovers!
Not for them a uniform of dull khaki — they are
the beehived, bouffanted, back-combed, permed,

straightened, lipsticked, perfumed, polished,
padded, dyed, lightened, feathered, pencilled,
glitter-eared, pearl-throated, jewel-fingered,

clipped, corested and cinched-in front-line troops;
who stand and serve however fierce the battle,
who honour their pledges, rarely falter at their posts;

who separate rebel factions, mop spittle and blood,
who have marched out scoundrels and cowards,
with the rapid gunfire of their wit, have seen off

the slovenly and big-headed and good-for-nowts
with a  blinding searchlight glare from flashing eyes,
a tongue-lashing that leaves each target shaking,

who have fought their own battles with husbands
and lovers, with wayward children, sisters, brothers
— patched up their wounds and returned to the front,

who have served loyally under fierce generals
and dishonest officers; who have offered comfort
to the shell-shocked, the battle-scarred, to those

who found themselves signed up to serve in wars
that spilled from kitchen to street, battered by
the bitterness of ancient feuds and grudges.

Let's raise a glass to these undaunted women,
whose medals are not brass, but diamante.
And leave at once when they holler closing time.

*Catherine Smith*

## Before The Flood

Down the Manhattan streets a man must go,
a man who is not himself Manhattan –
a tribe long gone and mostly forgotten.
Shaft by name and shaft by nurture,
he's no white knight, this brother,
neither marlowe nor mister tibbs.
This is blaxploitation not film noir
and its quippiest line is UP YOURS.
The words are clunky but the music's funky . .

*Shaft . . woo hoo . . Saviour of the Universe*

Or was that Star Trek? I loved Uhura.
She taught me that black was beautiful
years before Shaft said white was ugly –
the monstrous mob waddling into Harlem,
every wiseguy a Jabba the Pizzahut.
But that's just the way it goes I suppose,
every tribe rises by stomping on another,
by hurling names like weapons, hot
with the iron of the smelting pot –

the Jets and the Sharks, the Slants and the Schwartz
the Yids and the Micks, the Wops and the Spiks . .

But they're all black as ants
to the wasps looking down on them
from the nests in the topless towers.
On the high steel Hiawatha's in a hard hat
hammering the city's bones into place,
stonecold eyes in a stonecold face
watching the insects as he scrapes their skies,
unzipping his flies to wash the invaders away
with the fine gold rain of the Iroquois.

*Mike Dillon*

## Haikai-No-Renga for Inspector Harry Callahan

Rooftop swimming pool —
a bullet outstrips its own
bang! Silence again.

The gathering storm,
then thunder, lightning and rain —
fractured fire hydrant.

A chopper hovers
under the same cloud
where it hovered yesterday.

That kid had rights too —
the right to remain silent,
the right to remain.

Another man down —
the marble wall has a place
for his name, not yours.

Floodlit AstroTurf —
red carnations bloom again,
old wounds re-open.

The phones are ringing,
your ears ring even louder —
reverse the charges.

Insects never lie,
Inspector — she was long gone
before this began.

Beside the quarry,
the scorpion takes the bait —
gunfire and brimstone.

*Andrew J. Wilson*

## Audrey Hepburn

War child, in Arnhem
a world of soldiers, growling tanks,
knowledge a rat inside her.

Sugar frosting slick, and opaque,
on Capote's sour cherry.
Celluloid swims, then fixes its crystal eye:
a girl sits, chewing
outside a jeweller's shop.
Her name is Audrey
and you've never seen her before.

Later, famous, meeting her father,
a distant shore
her feelings can't wash over.

Then, in Africa, crow's feet on a goddess,
thin wrists whipped around
a dying baby.
In her silences, you can hear
the ghosts of Arnhem;
in her heart, tank divisions
still roll through its streets.

*Andrew C Ferguson*

# Bringing up Kathy

What must it be like to be a hunting, shooting, fishing, talking, skating, golfing, smoking,
riding, horsing kind of girl?

What must it be like to go skinny-dipping in the fountain pool at Bryn Mawr, to be so
sure you'd miss all the fun if you obey all the rules?

To never hesitate, or give the appearance of never hesitating? To leap, roll, pratfall
on screen, in life, wrestling with a leopard just out of diapers,

the leopard inside that chews all the abstracts—fame, faith, philosophy—
as if cutting
spectacular teeth?

It must be sublime, of course, until the day the *me me me* of me yields to the you-ness of
you. Kath puts it best: LOVE has nothing

to do with what you are expecting to get—only with what you are expecting to give—
which is everything.

*Jane McKie*

## Gåta

Kurt a Scotch in his claustral flat sips.
The bare case facts a mind order
in him improvise.

Elsewhere seems to be all happening:
in Nyberg's brain *overtimed*, in Linda's
love life *overturned*

at the locus *lacklustre* of the latest crime.
Deceived, dear viewer, do not be:
Waken Wallander will

to critical skelf evidence long
overlooked or scurried from his team
in nick of time.

Later, no/sooner, no. Is this what we demand
of a detective *braw* on a Saturday night:
That he be dour

as winter in Ystad; That a monkish
silence he maintain in the bulk
of scenes; That

the whole world rotten he bang
to rights by the closing credits; That he us
in turn turn in?

*Andrew Philip*

## Who Killed Morse?

It was a superior officer, in the station, with uncompleted paperwork
creased into a point,
a publican, at the fork in the past where the story began, with an
anagram,
a black-nailed, blackmailed mechanic, in the snug, with a flashback,
a mezzo, in the inspection pit, with a pint so badly kept he saw it seethe,
a don, in the wings of a student Parsifal, with a monkey-wrench,
a ritually dishevelled Mason, in a dreaming spire, with arias,
a crossword setter, in a temple, with the high-lit notes of a plagiarised
thesis,
a victim, in the dog ears of the dictionary, with a trowel.
It was a woman, who killed him from the inside out, with refusal.

*Julia Bird*

# The Method

*"I was a child nobody wanted. A lonely girl with a dream..." Marilyn Monroe*

There are ways of acting which can be taught;
if the actor uses The Method

it will look a lot like real life.  It may even
start to feel like that.  It is as plausible as a dream.

She wasn't an orphan.  She had a mother,
had a father, living in a mansion in Beverly Hills.

Sometimes she thinks: *If I was pretty enough,
my father would come and take me away.*

In the orphanage she stares through the window
at the distant neon

on top of the RKO lot,
sees it flash and thinks, *someday.*

A Method actor will do something false
until it becomes second nature.  That way

they will not be playing at it.  No-one
will be able to tell the difference.  Perhaps the actor

will not be able to tell the difference either.
Sometimes, if a life is awful enough,

there will be comfort in this.  A doctor says: *Child,
save your tears!  You may need them.*

*(from the writing of Alastair McKay)*

*Brian Johnstone*

## Always Ours

She shared the molten swagger of Monroe
but was no frayed paper goddess. This *Siren*

*of Swindon*, her honeyed hair falling thick
as a cat's purr. Later, she swooned on chat shows,

brought light to rainy afternoons. The fatal stab
of cancer got her in the end. She left a secret fortune,

a husband haunted by the ice-ache of her loss.
One October morning pointing a gun at his brow,

he joined her. It took code breakers to crack the cipher
she chose to hide her millions. Diana was always

ours, she was no Monroe. Nothing shaking
that canny head from it's broad blond shoulders.

*Naomi Woddis*

## The Man from U.N.C.L.E

Don't tell me I am only Illya Kuryakin
You don't know the first thing about
Being an intellectual undercover agent.

And yes, so what if Napoleon Solo
Always got the girl?
What are you implying?
What should I infer from your jibes?

Not every man you meet will be
Capable of communicating via a pen,
Not every man you meet will
Protect you from *Thrush.*

So unless you want this cold war
To go on between us, ignore
The supposed hidden meaning
Of my lemon triangular No 2.
I am waiting for no man.
In Japan yellow signifies courage
And in some cultures peace.

Don't tell me I'm only Ilya Kuryakin.
Cease dismissing me as a sidekick.
Come from behind your iron curtain,
I am more stereotypically Dostoeyevsky
Than *Dos ve danya , aishiteru yo, mi amor*
Meet me at the most exotic location
You can think of and we will re-create
On a suitable backlot, in a number of acts
The poly-lingual language of requited love.

*Kevin Cadwallender*

## Sapphire and Steel

Elemental
They arrive in shadow
A procession
Of the lambent
Summoned
With plague nursery rhymes
Innocence
Tempted by wraiths

In a whisper of blue
And the tang of alloy
They stand at the centre
Of the unheard

Gawping children
Like stopped clocks,
Night wings of moths
Fidget in their guts

Sapphire, a virtuoso
Conducting time.
Steel, the key
Unlocking sleep.

*Deborah Murray*

## Anne Bancroft Addresses the No-Name Ladies' Lunch

*I haven't the* . . . she began,
but exactly what she had not got
eluded her and she laughed
and shook her head
in that way she had,
that everyone, including me,
had loved her for,
for years and years
and she began again: *I haven't the* . . .
And everyone, including me, who loved her
knew she had it
even if she no longer knew
exactly what it was.

*Annie Freud*

# Mel Brooks

Hey, Kaminsky, Tummler, (kluge) klutz,
Der Guten Tag Hop Clop is so you
Working that red black and white uniform look so well
That outsider-antihero leitmotif.
Yeah, scrawny Brooklyn kike kid, you made good, already.
No one  bullies you now, Kaminsky.

Saved yourself with one-liners
Deflected punches with punchlines
You made us love monsters,
Rewrote the sacred cow(boy) movie
Got us to sing with Adolf in the Chinese Theatre.

Did those years in the Catskills hone that bone dry satire?
Then topped it off nicely on TV
A decade of plausible bumbling with Carl Reiner.
Did you cut your teeth on Get Smart?
Don Adams in a sharp suit
You, Mr Sharp-tongue.

Officially Mr Comedian's Comedian
Monarch of the musical.
They went wild for you and Wilder
Grammys Emmys Tonys, Oscar
The whole schmeer

You got the girl Kaminsky
Married Anne in Manhattan
The outsider came in
The unlikely schmuck triumphed
And how!

What a guy!

What a Production!

*Carolyn P Richardson*

## The Library of Bronze
*variation on a theme by Orhan Pamuk*

One night all the statues of Burns
came to life at the one unannointed moment.
There was a worldwide squeal of necks
in doubletake at where he found himself,
then down he stepped into small towns
so far from understanding
they hid in their houses as he clanked down
thin streets looking for a bar or garage
serving some kind of necessary oil
and wishing he had been equestrian.

Part-Talos, part tale-teller,
he habbied through fences and forests,
fording single oceans in a series of rhetorical leaps;
part-author, part-Terminator
he flyted unquaking Shakespeares
and clasped the hands of a legion of Pushkins
before congregating in the town of his birth,
all its flesh inhabitants having fled
beyond the toughened tourist fence
to sell tickets and telescopes.

And there the statues lived in promiscuity
with fridges and washing machines,
meeting nightly to compare
verses scratched on the bonnets
and in the windscreens of cars
cannibalised into their vast library,
each written in bronze's incomprehensible dialect –
undoubtedly addressed to you, his rusty fiere,
but, as they debated, could these all be by
the same awoken Bard?

*W N Herbert*

## the king of monsters takes a break

out on the endless machair
they fly in as a white caterwaul
the name clutched in their shrieking beaks
*gojira! gojira!*
the west coast of scotland they say
is his favoured getaway destination
those long empty beaches
a balm for the overworked saurian

he lolls in the waves
at an unnamed destination
somewhere between barvas and boreray
the sky spills rain as if an illness
the water runs from his scales
in a chorus of burns
he likes the isolation he says
(we communicate telepathically)
a break from the ruination
the constant in-fighting
mothra and all those other guys

he has a pylon or perhaps a girder
wedged in his left foot
a remnant from kicking his way
through some power station or other
his eyes roll back in his head
*could you help me with that*
so i go and fetch choinneach's digger
it being a sunday he'll have a bad head
hitch the mixer to the back so i can cement
the wound with bone sand and atlantic salt
it's heavy work and a welcome beer
when it's done

godzilla looks out to the clisham
out across the blue waters

he likes the gaelic singing he says
it makes him feel like a cloud
weightless, away from all those cities
in flame, the constant sting of helicopters
warning sirens, the roar of bombs
he tells me that down there
in the ocean dark he enjoys
the composition of haiku
but there's always a submarine
to torpedo his train of thought

*a change of scene* he says
shaking his massive head
disturbing the cool drape of weed
in a blur of angry terns
*a change of scene is what i need*
i look deep into the reptilian iris
down into the great ache of his heart
and i say, have you ever considered glasgow?

*Morgan Downie*

## Closedown

The incunabula of television,
Crystal Palace, lipstick and clipped tones,
Muffin the Mule, then finally the flicks
crammed into tubes, inferior Bibles, cloned,
invaded all our evenings. *Television
will kill the Cinema!* doom-pundits cried,
erroneously. We, mesmerised, pie-eyed,
in small square post-utility sitting rooms,
witnessed the small square triumph of the box,
Stevenson's toy theatre, exaggerating life.
Coach became pumpkin at eleven o'clock,
rooms shrank, books closed, bare remnants of the plot.
*Goodnight. Remember to switch off your set.*
The screen collapsed into a small white dot.

*Sally Evans*

## The White Dot

A blink of frenzy on the living room screen as rescuers
haul the last known survivor from reinforced dust

where her house once stood: at over 100 years old
she's already witness and survivor of more

than most would care to imagine, especially the young
reporter who, elsewhere in the stricken province, presses

a cordless phone into the hands of a trapped man so she
can beam his last conversation round the franchised globe

as his voice falters and gives out. On another channel
someone's claiming to speak to the dead between adverts

but who can really tell if anybody's there to listen
and whether after is so much better than before?

Meantime, in a stricken province elsewhere, the masses
have gathered to stake their claim on the hearse of a poet

and his refusal to be shackled by facts on the ground
or factions growing fat on such bloody sterilities

while viewers in the starstruck provinces ask
the big questions of the day, such as: How <u>do</u> you

solve a problem like Maria? Some say
it's all about the sense of scale and why you should

be a socialist, but each of us switches off eventually
like an old cathode ray television set, its picture

dwindling to that tiny white dot before the blackness. (Now
it's all so slick: sleek flat LCD sets in front rooms,

great big plasma screens dotted about the city —
nothing to fixate on as the box powers down.)

*Andrew Philip*

85

## About the Editor

The choice of poetic themes reflects the fascinations of compiler and editor **Andy Jackson**.

Andy Jackson is from Manchester, but moved to east Fife twenty years ago, settling in Dundee. He is a Medical Librarian at the University of Dundee. His poetry has been published in a variety of magazines including *New Writing Scotland, Magma, Blackbox Manifold, Gutter, Rising and Northwords Now.* He won the National Galleries of Scotland Creative Writing competition in 2008. His first collection, *The Assassination Museum,* was published by Red Squirrel Press in 2010 (ISBN 978906700164), described by Ian McMillan as "alive with possibility and excitement". A second collection is forthcoming.